FREE DVD

/D

Essential Test Tips DVD from Trivium Test Prep

Dear Customer,

Thank you for purchasing from Cirrus Test Prep! Whether you're looking to join the military, get into college, or advance your career, we're honored to be a part of your journey.

To show our appreciation (and to help you relieve a little of that test-prep stress), we're offering a **FREE** ***Praxis Essential Test Tips DVD**** by Cirrus Test Prep. Our DVD includes 35 test preparation strategies that will help keep you calm and collected before and during your big exam. All we ask is that you email us your feedback and describe your experience with our product. Amazing, awful, or just so-so: we want to hear what you have to say!

To receive your **FREE** ***Praxis Essential Test Tips DVD***, please email us at 5star@cirrustestprep.com. Include "Free 5 Star" in the subject line and the following information in your email:

1. The title of the product you purchased.
2. Your rating from 1 – 5 (with 5 being the best).
3. Your feedback about the product, including how our materials helped you meet your goals and ways in which we can improve our products.
4. Your full name and shipping address so we can send your **FREE** ***Praxis Essential Test Tips DVD***.

If you have any questions or concerns please feel free to contact us directly at 5star@cirrustestprep.com. Thank you, and good luck with your studies!

* Please note that the free DVD is <u>not included</u> with this book. To receive the free DVD, please follow the instructions above.

Praxis II Social Studies (5081) Rapid Review Flash Cards

TEST PREP INCLUDING 450+ FLASH CARDS FOR THE PRAXIS 5081 EXAM

Table of Contents

Introduction i

US History 1

World History 69

Government 171

Geography 205

Economics 239

Sociology 273

Psychology 291

Introduction

Congratulations on choosing to take the Praxis Social Studies: Content Knowledge (5081) exam! By purchasing this book, you've taken the first step toward becoming a social studies teacher.

This guide will provide you with a detailed overview of the Praxis, so you know exactly what to expect on test day. We'll take you through all the concepts covered on the test and give you the opportunity to test your knowledge with practice questions. Even if it's been a while since you last took a major test, don't worry; we'll make sure you're more than ready!

What is the Praxis?

Praxis Series tests are a part of teaching licensure in approximately forty states. Each state uses the tests and scores in different ways, so be sure to check the certification requirements in your state by going to www.ets.org/praxis/states. There, you will find information detailing the role of the Praxis tests in determining teaching certification in your state, what scores are required, and how to transfer Praxis scores from one state to another.

The social studies tests are interdisciplinary; they test your ability to understand relationships among fields in social studies. These include US and world history, US government/civics, economics, geography, and behavioral sciences. You'll integrate your knowledge of all of these subjects in order to answer the questions correctly.

What's on the Praxis?

The content in this guide will prepare you for the Praxis Social Studies: Content Knowledge (5081) exam. This multiple-choice test assesses whether you possess the knowledge and skills necessary to become a secondary school social studies teacher. You have a maximum of two hours to complete the entire test. The test always has a total of 130 multiple-choice questions; however, the number of questions specific to each subject is approximate (see the table below).

Praxis Social Studies: Content Knowledge (5081) Content		
Concepts	**Approximate Number of Questions**	**Percentage**
US History	26	20%
World History	26	20%
Government/Civics	26	20%
Economics	19	15%
Geography	19	15%
Behavioral Sciences	13	10%
Total	**Always 130**	**2 hours**

You will answer approximately twenty-six multiple-choice questions (20 percent of the test) on United States history. The test will require knowledge of North American geography, pre-colonial civilizations, the purposes of European colonization of the continent, and how pre-colonial peoples interacted with European colonizers. Be prepared for questions about the American Revolution and the foundations of the United States government and Constitution. The test will cover developments in the nineteenth century, including westward expansion, political division, the Civil War, Reconstruction, industrialization, urbanization, and immigration. The Progressive Era and the New Deal are covered as well. Be aware not only of United States involvement in the First and Second World Wars, but also of their impact on both foreign and domestic policy. Prepare for thematic questions that will test your knowledge of the impact of labor and technology on the economy, changing political trends from the New Deal and Great Society to conservatism, the impact of religion on society, and civil rights and changing perceptions of race, ethnicity and gender roles throughout the twentieth century. Questions are also likely to explore the United States' role as a world power during the Cold War and into the twenty-first century.

You will answer approximately twenty-six multiple-choice questions (20 percent of the test) on world history. In general, you will be expected to understand how world societies and civilizations have been shaped by conflict, technology, and religion; ideologies like nationalism, totalitarianism and other political philosophies; economic movements like industrialization and the market economy; and major demographic trends. It will also presume an understanding of trans-global similarities in gender and family expectations, and the impact of trade within and among cultures. Specific questions may ask about the classical civilizations in Europe and Asia and their transformation from 300 – 1400 C.E.; European developments from the Renaissance through the Enlightenment; colonization, trade, and other global interactions from 1200 – 1750 C.E.; the consequences of nationalism and European imperialism from 1750 – 1914 C.E.; the causes and consequences of the First and Second World Wars (like decolonization and the rise of the Soviet Union); and the important developments of the post-Cold War world (such as globalization and fundamentalism).

You will answer approximately twenty-six multiple-choice questions (20 percent of the test) on government, politics, and civics. Generally, you will need to have a solid understanding of major political concepts, orientations, and theorists. United States government, its constitutional foundation, national political institutions, and its three branches of government will be covered on the test. You will also be assessed on your knowledge of how national political institutions' processes, structures, and powers function. Expect questions about the effects of civil rights, political ideology, political parties, special interest groups, and the media on politics. In addition to domestic US government, you'll be asked questions about comparative politics and international relations. The test will presume knowledge of the types of government, such as parliamentary and federal; in addition, prepare to be asked about types of regimes, such as democracies, autocracies, and oligarchies. International relations will be tested on a theoretical and practical level: for example, how theory relates to cooperation among nations and diplomacy in practice. You'll also be tested on the powers and problems of international laws and organizations, such as NATO and the United Nations.

You will answer approximately nineteen multiple-choice questions (15 percent of the test) on economics. The test will assess the two major content areas of economics: micro and macro. Questions about the former cover concepts such as economic systems, distribution of income, behavior of firms, product markets, market efficiency, governmental controls, factors of production, and choice and opportunity costs. Macroeconomics questions ask about measures of economic performance, fiscal and monetary policies, money and banking, inflation and economic growth, exchange rates and international trade, business cycles, and unemployment.

You will answer approximately nineteen multiple-choice questions (15 percent of the test) on geography. Questions will not only ask you to glean information from maps, projections, and geographical data, but also to analyze and organize this information in conjunction with your own spatial understanding and mental maps. You will be asked to identify patterns and interpret data from a variety of sources and to display your understanding of concepts like political geography, state formation, and contemporary areas of conflict. An understanding of human geography is also essential to this section. Prepare to answer questions about demographic patterns and change. The test will also cover interrelationships of humans and their environments and how culture, economics, migration and settlement, development, industrialization, and globalization affect those relationships.

You will answer approximately thirteen multiple-choice questions (10 percent of the test) on behavioral sciences. Behavioral sciences questions focus on human behavior and its influencing factors: these include learning, identity, and development as well as society, social groups, and institutions. The test will also cover how culture, diversity, and adaptation affect human behavior.

How is the Praxis Scored?

The multiple-choice questions are equally weighted. Keep in mind that some multiple-choice questions are experimental questions for the purpose of the Praxis test writers and will not count toward your overall score. However, since those questions are not indicated on the test, you must respond to every question. There is no penalty for guessing on Praxis tests, so be sure to eliminate answer choices and answer every question. If you still do not know the answer, guess; you may get it right!

Your score report will be available on your Praxis account for one year, but you can also opt for a paper report. The score report includes your score and the passing score for the states you identified as score recipients. Your score will be available immediately after the test.

How is the Praxis Administered?

The Praxis Series tests are available at testing centers across the nation. To find a testing center near you, go to http://www.ets.org/praxis/register. At this site, you can create a Praxis account, check testing dates, register for a test, or find instructions for registering via mail or phone. The Praxis Social Studies: Content Knowledge (5081) exam is administered as a computerized test. The Praxis website allows you to take a practice test to acclimate yourself to the computerized format.

On the day of your test, be sure to bring your admission ticket (which is provided when you register) and photo ID. The testing facility will provide pencils and erasers and an area outside of the testing room to store your personal belongings. You are allowed no personal effects in the testing area. Cell phones and other electronic, photographic, recording, or listening devices are not permitted in the testing center at all, and bringing those items may be cause for dismissal, forfeiture of your testing fees, and cancellation of your scores. For details on what is and is not permitted at your testing center, refer to http://www.ets.org/praxis/test_day/bring.

About Cirrus Test Prep

Cirrus Test Prep study guides are designed by current and former educators and are tailored to meet your needs as an incoming educator. Our guides offer all of the resources necessary to help you pass teacher certification tests across the nation.

Cirrus clouds are graceful, wispy clouds characterized by their high altitude. Just like cirrus clouds, Cirrus Test Prep's goal is to help educators "aim high" when it comes to obtaining their teacher certification and entering the classroom.

About This Guide

This guide will help you master the most important test topics and also develop critical test-taking skills. We have built features into our books to prepare you for your tests and increase your score. Along with a detailed summary of the test's format, content, and scoring, we offer an in-depth overview of the content knowledge required to pass the test. Our sidebars provide interesting information, highlight key concepts, and review content so that you can solidify your understanding of the exam's concepts. Test your knowledge with sample questions and detailed answer explanations in the text that help you think through the problems on the exam and two full-length practice tests that reflect the content and format of the Praxis. We're pleased you've chosen Cirrus to be a part of your professional journey!

US History

encomienda system

Columbian Exchange

the Spanish system for controlling and exploiting land and labor in the Western Hemisphere

describes the broad exchange of people, ideas, organisms, and technology across the Atlantic (encompassing *triangular trade*)

triangular trade

mercantilism

Iroquois Confederacy

refers to the pattern of trade in the Atlantic world; Europeans purchased or kidnapped Africans in West Africa to be enslaved, taken to the Americas, and traded for raw materials like sugar; these materials were taken to Europe and traded for consumer goods; and these goods were exchanged in Africa for slaves (and sometimes also in the colonies)

economic system in which the colonizing country took raw materials from colonies for its own benefit, amassing wealth through protectionism and increasing exports at the expense of other rising colonial powers

Established before European contact, the Iroquois Confederacy, or League, was a union of five tribes: the Mohawk, Onondaga, Oneida, Cayuga, and Seneca.

Algonquin

Cherokee

Creek, Chickasaw, and Choctaw

northeastern Native American civilization in the Great Lakes region

Southeastern Native American civilization thought to be descended from the Iroquois; emerged in present-day Georgia; forced during the Trail of Tears to leave their land and migrate to Indian Territory (Oklahoma)

major Muskogean-speaking southeastern Native American civilizations; descendants of the Mississippi Mound Builders

Shawnee

Plains tribes

Navajo

an Algonquin-speaking people based in the Ohio Valley; the Shawnee leader Tecumseh led the Northwest Confederacy against the United States in 1812

included the Sioux, Cheyenne, Apache, Comanche, and Arapaho who lived in the Great Plains area; nomadic peoples; depended mainly on the buffalo for sustenance

a pastoral people that controlled territory in present-day Arizona, New Mexico, and Utah; descendants of the Ancestral Pueblo, or Anasazi, who built cliff dwellings

maroon communities

Halfway Covenant

Maryland Toleration Act

settlements of escaped slaves in the Western Hemisphere

a 1662 policy that allowed membership in the Puritan Church for children and grandchildren of members if they promised to live by the tenets of the church; however, they would not have voting rights in it

1649 law ensuring the political rights of all Christians in Maryland; the first law of its kind in the colonies

salutary neglect

Proclamation of 1763

Quartering Act

long-standing British policy of autonomy toward the colonies until the mid-eighteenth century

issued by King George III in 1763; drew a line of demarcation along the Appalachian Mountains past which colonists were forbidden

a 1765 law that forced American colonists to provide shelter, even in their homes, to British troops stationed in the region; important trigger for colonial discontent

Stamp Act

Boston Massacre

Tea Act

controversial 1765 tax on all published documentation in the Colonies; the first direct tax on the colonists; major source of colonial discontent

1770 event in which British troops fired on a crowd of American protestors; important controversy leading to revolution

controversial 1773 tax on colonial tea that triggered the Boston Tea Party

Boston Tea Party

Intolerable Acts

First Continental Congress

1773 protest of the Tea Act in which American colonial protestors disguised as Native Americans tossed tea off a ship in Boston Harbor

1774 acts enforced by Britain in response to tensions and violence in the colonies, including closing Boston Harbor and bringing Massachusetts back under direct royal control

meeting of colonial leaders in Philadelphia in 1774, organized in response to the Intolerable Acts; colonial leaders later presented concerns to the king and were rebuffed

George Washington

Thomas Jefferson

Sons and Daughters of Liberty

colonial military leader, general of the Continental Army, first US president; his able military leadership helped the colonies eventually secure independence, and his political leadership helped keep the young country united

colonial leader, architect of the Declaration of Independence; third US president; Jefferson was an anti-Federalist and disapproved of a strong US Constitution

colonial rebel protest group that carried out violent acts against tax collectors

John Adams

Samuel Adams

Committees of Correspondence

colonial leader, member of the Continental Congress, federalist, second US president, brother to the radical Samuel Adams; Adams supported a strong federal government and expanded executive power

radical colonial American rebel; leader of the Sons and Daughters of Liberty and Committees of Correspondence

colonial rebel protest group that distributed anti-British propaganda

Declaration of Independence

Battles of Lexington and Concord

Battle of Bunker Hill

Issued on July 4, 1776, this document, written in great part by Thomas Jefferson and signed by the leaders of the Second Continental Congress, asserted US independence from Britain; it later influenced other independence movements worldwide.

beginning of violent conflict between American rebel militiamen (minutemen) and the British in 1775

took place on June 17, 1775; caused King George III to declare that the colonies were in rebellion

Battle of Yorktown

Second Continental Congress

Shays' Rebellion

1781 defeat of British forces by the Continental Army with support from France, ending the Revolutionary War

meeting of colonial leaders in Philadelphia in 1775 where colonial leaders agreed on declaring independence and forming the United States of America

revolt of indebted farmers protesting government property seizures in Massachusetts and debtors' prisons; an indication that the US federal government needed to be strengthened

Constitutional Convention

Bill of Rights

Federalist Papers

1787 meeting of the states to resolve problems arising from limitations on federal power; states abandoned the Articles of Confederation and developed the Constitution, strengthening the federal government

the first ten amendments to the US Constitution; a set of guarantees of certain rights enjoyed by Americans; incentive for anti-Federalists to agree to the Constitution, which strengthened the federal government

essays by Alexander Hamilton, James Madison, and John Jay articulating the benefits of federalism and written to convince the states to ratify the Constitution

Three-Fifths Compromise

President Washington's Farewell Address

Louisiana Purchase

the decision to count a slave as three-fifths of a person to determine a state's representation in Congress; enslaved persons had no voice in the political process

In a published address at the end of his presidency, Washington recommended the United States follow a policy of neutrality in international affairs, setting a precedent for early American history.

controversial 1803 purchase of French-controlled territory in North America by the United States, authorized by President Jefferson; nearly doubled the size of the country

War of 1812

Second Great Awakening

Manifest Destiny

This conflict pitted the US against Britain and the British-allied Northwest Confederacy (led by the Shawnee leader Tecumseh). Despite British attacks from Canada, the US maintained its territorial integrity and gained power in the Northwest (present-day Ohio Valley region), facilitating westward expansion.

a period of religious revival in which people turned from Puritanism and predestination to Baptist and Methodist faiths, among others, following revolutionary preachers and movements

the concept that it was the mission and fate of the United States to expand westward and settle the continent

Monroe Doctrine

Tariff of Abominations

Nullification Crisis

President James Monroe's policy closing off the Western Hemisphere to any further European colonization or exploration, asserting US hegemony in the region

passed in order to protect and promote the growth of Northern industries; officially called the Tariff of 1828, it was known as the Tariff of Abominations by its Southern detractors, who relied on international trade

Faced with the Tariff of 1828, or Tariff of Abominations, Southern states argued that a state had the right to declare a law null and void if it was harmful to that state.

Indian Removal Act

Trail of Tears

nativism

1830 law that forced Cherokee, Creek, Chickasaw, Choctaw, and others from their lands in the southeast to Indian Territory (Oklahoma)

the forced migration of Cherokee and others from their lands in the southeast to Indian Territory (today, Oklahoma) to make way for white settlers, following the Indian Removal Act; the term describes the suffering and poor conditions endured by many during the migration

nineteenth-century, anti-immigrant movement, particularly anti-Catholic; politicized by the Know-Nothing Party

Missouri Compromise (Compromise of 1820)

Fugitive Slave Act

Compromise of 1850

allowed Missouri to join the union as a slave state, provided that any other states north of the thirty-sixth parallel ($36^0 30'$) would be free; Maine would also join the nation as a free state

allowed slave owners to pursue escaped slaves to free states and recapture them

admitted the populous California as a free state and Utah and New Mexico to the Union, with slavery to be decided by popular sovereignty; also strengthened and reaffirmed the Fugitive Slave Act

Kansas-Nebraska Act

Scott v. Sandford

abolitionism

1854 act that permitted the question of slavery to be decided by popular sovereignty in the Kansas Territory, even though it was north of the thirty-sixth parallel, in conflict with the Missouri Compromise

1856 Supreme Court case brought by Dred Scott; upheld the Fugitive Slave Act, the Kansas-Nebraska Act, and nullified the Missouri Compromise, essentially finding that African Americans were not entitled to rights under US citizenship

the ending of slavery

Underground Railroad

Battle of Fort Sumter

Emancipation Proclamation

a secret network of safe houses and connections to help Southern slaves escape to the North and to Canada

1861 attack on Union troops in Sumter, South Carolina, by Confederate forces shortly after South Carolina seceded from the Union; this battle sparked the Civil War

January 1, 1863, declaration by President Lincoln abolishing slavery in the US rebel states

Abraham Lincoln

Frederick Douglass

Radical Republicans

first Republican president, an abolitionist elected in 1860; his election triggered Southern secession; led the country through the Civil War but was assassinated in 1865 before Reconstruction truly began

advocate for abolition, writer, activist, and former slave himself; publicized the abolitionist movement

advocated for equal rights for blacks during Reconstruction

Homestead Act of 1862

Dawes Act

Elizabeth Cady Stanton

granted 160 acres of land in the West to any settler who promised to settle and work it for a number of years, accelerating settlement

in 1887, ended federal recognition of tribes, withdrew tribal land rights, forced the sale of tribal land; also sent Native children to harmful boarding schools where they were forced to abandon their languages and cultures

women's rights activist; founded the National Woman Suffrage Association and led the 1848 Seneca Falls Convention on women's rights

Susan B. Anthony

Transcontinental Railroad

assembly line

women's rights activist and leader in women's suffrage movement; leader at 1848 Seneca Falls Convention

built between 1863 and 1869, the First Transcontinental Railroad connected the Pacific Coast to the Atlantic Coast for the first time

a labor-intensive method of production developed by Henry Ford in which workers repetitively execute separate key tasks in production, expediting the completion of a product

labor unions

Progressive Movement

sharecropping

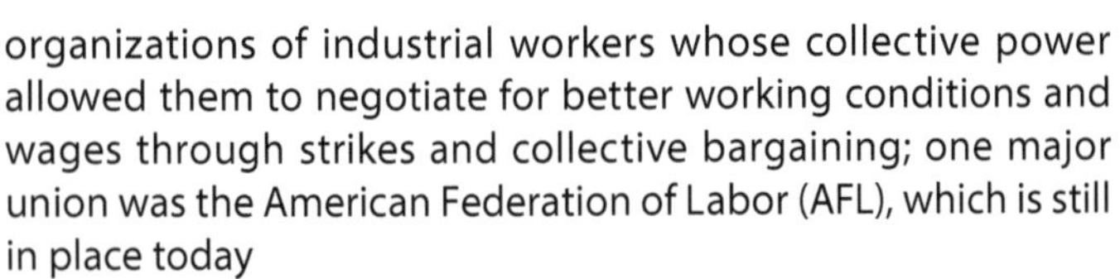

organizations of industrial workers whose collective power allowed them to negotiate for better working conditions and wages through strikes and collective bargaining; one major union was the American Federation of Labor (AFL), which is still in place today

refers to the work of an alliance of advocates for the rights of workers, women, and immigrants in the early twentieth century; resulted in legislation that protected public health, the environment, workers, and children under Presidents Roosevelt and Taft

agricultural system in the South in which many freed slaves worked the same land for the same landowners, leasing land and equipment at unreasonable rates, essentially trapped in the same conditions they had lived in before emancipation

Plessy v. Ferguson

yellow journalism

Roosevelt Corollary to the Monroe Doctrine

1896 case in which the Supreme Court upheld segregation in the Southern states

in the late nineteenth and early twentieth centuries, sensationalized and exaggerated media coverage that stirred up popular unrest, especially in regard to US entry into the Spanish-American War

Theodore Roosevelt's assertion of the US as a global military power; promised US military intervention in Latin America in case of European intervention there

“Peace without Victory”

Bonus March

Great Depression

On January 22, 1917, shortly before entering into World War I, President Woodrow Wilson made a speech to the United States Senate calling for "peace without victory" in the European conflict.

In 1932, 17,000 World War I veterans and their families marched on the Capitol and the White House to demand payment for the bonus certificates they received for their efforts during the war.

the global economic collapse that resulted in widespread poverty and unemployment in the United States and the world

Franklin Delano Roosevelt (FDR)

New Deal

Lend-Lease Act

elected to the presidency in 1932; developed the New Deal, rescuing the United States from the Great Depression, and led the country through World War II

plan presented by FDR to rescue the United States from the Great Depression; included emergency acts to save the banking system and long-term relief for the poor and unemployed

the 1941 act that allowed Great Britain and its allies to receive food and oil, and to borrow ships and other war equipment; in exchange, the US was leased army and naval bases in Allied territory, enabling it to transport war equipment to Europe long before it entered WWII

Four Freedoms

Pearl Harbor

D-Day

In the context of the rise of fascism, FDR defined these as freedom of speech, freedom of religion, freedom from want, and freedom from fear.

US military base in Hawaii; in December 1941, Japan attacked Pearl Harbor, causing the US to enter WWII

June 6, 1944, when the US led the invasion of Normandy, invading Europe during WWII

Cold War

arms race

containment

period of ongoing tension and conflict between the US and the USSR, the post–WWII global superpowers; remained "cold" because the two countries never engaged in direct military confrontation

competitive weapons development between the US and the USSR during the 1980s; the US intended to outspend the USSR, thereby weakening it

the US policy toward the Soviet Union at the beginning of the Cold War that focused on preventing the USSR from increasing its sphere of influence

iron curtain

Brown v. Board of Education

War on Poverty

a metaphor for the concept of a post–WWII Europe divided between east (with communist governments generally aligned with the USSR) and west (with democratic capitalist governments generally aligned with the US)

1954 Supreme Court case that ended segregation of public schools, overturning precedent set by *Plessy v. Ferguson* and strengthening the growing civil rights movement

President Lyndon B. Johnson's movement to support the poor through government programs; resulted in legislation such as the Medicare Act, the creation of the Department of Housing and Urban Development, the Head Start program, and the Elementary and Secondary Education Act

Civil Rights Movement

Rev. Dr. Martin Luther King Jr.

Cesar Chavez

refers to the social and political movement for the rights of African Americans, women, and other disenfranchised people in the 1960s

civil rights leader who fought for equal rights for African Americans; embraced peaceful protest as a means to end segregation and to achieve legislative and social change

civil rights activist; led the United Farm Workers, which advocated for Hispanic farmworkers who faced racial discrimination, poor treatment, and low pay

Malcolm X

Warren Court

silent majority

civil rights leader who championed better living standards for blacks in northern cities and the empowerment of African American communities

From 1953 to 1969, the Supreme Court was under the direction of Chief Justice Earl Warren; during this time the court had a liberal majority that actively used its judicial power to bring about significant legal and cultural changes.

term coined by Richard Nixon in 1969 to refer to the majority of Americans who did not support the protest movements or counterculture of the 1960s

Watergate scandal

Reagan Era

September 11, 2001

named for the hotel where the Democratic National Committee offices were located and burglarized by a team connected to President Richard Nixon; led to Nixon's resignation

refers to the post-Watergate rejuvenation of conservatism during the 1981 – 1989 term of the popular Republican president Ronald Reagan, who increased military spending, implemented tax cuts, and embraced conservative social values

the date the United States was attacked by terrorists, resulting in thousands of civilian casualties and leading to lengthy land wars in Afghanistan and Iraq

preemption

Barack Obama

foreign policy doctrine of President George W. Bush; the US should preemptively attack the source of any threats to its national security; drove the 2003 invasion of Iraq under the premise that Iraq had weapons of mass destruction threatening the US

first African American president, elected in 2008; ended wars in Afghanistan and Iraq; halted the Great Recession; developed programs to provide healthcare to uninsured Americans

World History

East African slave trade

Queen Victoria

Arabs, Asians, and other Africans kidnapped African people and enslaved them throughout the Arab world and South Asia; later, Europeans did the same in African, Asian, and Indian Ocean colonies.

eighteenth-century British monarch who oversaw imperial expansion throughout India, Australia, and large parts of Africa

Napoleon Bonaparte

Songhai Empire

Fertile Crescent

nineteenth-century French emperor who conquered much of Europe, changing political balance of power on the continent

west-central African empire; succeeded the Mali Empire; rich in salt

the region stretching from the Persian Gulf through the land around the Tigris and Euphrates Rivers (Mesopotamia), the Levant (east coast of the Mediterranean Sea), and parts of the Nile Valley; with the first populations dating back to 10,000 BCE, the Fertile Crescent is thought to be the birthplace of the key aspects of civilization

Holocaust

Code of Hammurabi

Great Fear

the dispossession, imprisonment, and murder of at least six million Jews, Roma and Slavic people, homosexuals, disabled people, people of color, prisoners of war, communists, and others by the Nazis

one of the earliest-known codes of law; developed by the Babylonian king Hammurabi around 1754 BCE; contains punishments based on the now well-known expression "an eye for an eye, a tooth for a tooth"

terror among French peasants in 1789 over food shortages and a suspected conspiracy against the Third Estate; one trigger of the French Revolution

tithe

Machu Picchu

Qur'an

percentage of earnings (10 percent) owed as taxes to the nobility by peasants in pre-revolutionary France

Inca citadel in the Andes

the holy book of Islam

United Nations

Habsburg dynasty

King Henry VIII

an international organization formed after World War II to prevent another world war, champion human rights, and uphold international security

powerful Catholic European ruling family that controlled Austria and Spain throughout the Thirty Years' War and beyond

sixteenth-century English monarch; rejected Catholicism; founder of the Church of England

indulgences

Punic Wars

Francisco Pizarro

promises that knights who fought in the Crusades would be forgiven for any sins committed in war and go to heaven

a series of wars fought between Carthage and Rome between 264 and 146 BCE

Spanish conquistador who defeated the Inca king Atahualpa, effectively beginning Spanish rule in the Andean region

Treaty of Versailles

Laws of Manu

William the Conqueror

the treaty that ended WWI, held Germany accountable for the entirety of the war, and brought economic hardship to the country by forcing it to pay reparations to the other powers

2,684 verses that comprise the guiding principles of religious and legal duty in Hinduism

Norman leader who invaded England in 1066, bringing more organization and feudal economy

pyramids

Axis

Napoleonic Wars

Egyptian burial tombs for pharaohs

the alliance of Germany, Italy, and Japan during WWII

series of early nineteenth-century wars between Napoleonic France and various European powers; ultimately resulted in new balance of power in Europe

Vikings

Renaissance

Ivan the Great

Scandinavian seafaring civilization that explored the North Atlantic and northern Europe; evidence indicates the Vikings traveled as far as the eastern Mediterranean

revival of learning, art, architecture, and philosophy in Europe, especially influenced by work from ancient Greece and Rome; triggered social change and backlash against the Catholic Church

Russian leader and monarch who defeated the Mongols to return Moscow and Slavic lands to Russian control in 1480; consolidated early Russian Empire

feudalism

serfs

nation-state

socioeconomic organization in medieval Europe; a hierarchy where land and protection were offered in exchange for loyalty

peasants who remained on fiefs ("tied to the land") under feudalism; farmed for lords and granted small plots of land for personal use; were entitled to the lords' protection but not obligated to fight; not slaves, but not truly free persons

sovereign territory ruled by an ethnic majority

vassals

pope

Bubonic (Black) Plague

swore loyalty (fealty) to lords under the feudal system; were rewarded with land; shared yield

the leader of the Catholic Church; in medieval Europe, also a powerful political leader

bacterial infection with global effects that killed a third of Europeans in the fourteenth century; led to broader social change

mass production

Congress of Vienna

King Louis XIV

large-scale production of consumer products (enabled by the assembly line and factories)

following defeat of Napoleon in 1815, the conference where Prussia, the Austro-Hungarian Empire, Russia, and Britain agreed on balance of power in Europe; the first real international peace conference; set the precedent for European political organization

seventeenth-century French monarch who consolidated the monarchy and disempowered the nobility; known as *the Sun King*

reparations

Ming dynasty

Counter-Reformation

costly financial compensation charged to Germany by the victors of WWI to cover the cost of the war; considered by some historians to be a factor in German decline, leading to the rise of the Nazi Party

reestablished ethnic Han Chinese control in fourteenth-century China following the Yuan period; oversaw expansion of Chinese power; fostered cultural development

attempts at reinforcing Catholic dominance throughout Europe during and after the Reformation in the wake of the Renaissance and related social change

the Torah

the Crusades

Sparta

the central text of Judaism; describes the origin of the Israelites and of the world

a series of holy wars launched by Christian Europeans against Muslims in the Holy Land (the Levant) following the decline of the Christian Byzantine Empire

ancient Greek military city-state

Magna Carta

steam engine

bourgeoisie (French Revolution)

English document that protected the property and rights of individuals; the basis for today's parliamentary system in that country; early version of a constitution

important machine for the Industrial Revolution; powered factories, allowing them to be built anywhere, not just near natural sources of energy like bodies of water

In eighteenth-century France, *bourgeoisie* referred to the emergent middle class which was growing powerful thanks to early capitalism. The bourgeoisie were not traditionally nobles or landowners under the feudal system; along with peasants, the bourgeoisie bore the brunt of taxation.

imperialism

Third Estate

Kingdom of Ghana

the possession and exploitation of land overseas

the middle class (bourgeoisie) and peasants (commoners) of pre-revolutionary France; those who bore the brunt of taxation

gold-rich kingdom in West Africa; important trading partner of North African Muslims on the Trans-Saharan trade routes

Industrial Revolution

Triple Alliance

Holy Land

nineteenth-century economic revolution beginning in Europe marked by mechanization in agriculture and transportation and the emergence of factories

alliance of Austria-Hungary, Germany, and Italy in the First World War (against Russia, the United Kingdom, and France, the *Triple Entente*)

term to describe the Levant, location of holy cities and sites important to the three major monotheistic religions (Judaism, Christianity, and Islam); often used in reference to the Crusades

Aztecs

Ivan the Terrible

system of alliances

militaristic Mesoamerican civilization that dominated Mexico and Central America before European contact

Russian monarch who expanded Russian territory into Europe; strengthened government and Russian Orthodox Christianity

the complicated diplomatic and military alliances among European powers that led to the outbreak and magnitude of World War I

Treaty of Westphalia

Battle of Tours (or Poitiers)

Inquisition

ended the Thirty Years' War in 1648; established the concept of state sovereignty and noninterference; considered to be the foundation of modern international relations

victory by Charles Martel in 732 CE that stopped Islamic incursions into Europe

a court established by the Roman Catholic Church tasked with eradicating heresies, including witchcraft and alchemy; in reality, punished non-Christians, including Jews and Muslims, who refused to convert to Christianity

Umayyad Caliphate

genocide

guillotine

a Muslim empire based in Damascus; emerged from the Muslim conquest of the Arabian Peninsula; encompassed 5.8 million square miles; marked by stability, cultural and commercial growth, and tolerance of the "People of the Book" (Christians and Jews) as well as, in practice, Zoroastrians

killing people based on their ethnicity

device used by the republican government to execute counter-revolutionaries in post-revolutionary France; symbolic of chaotic period during the Reign of Terror

Yuan dynasty

Jean-Jacques Rousseau

knights

Mongol dynasty in China; upended local hierarchy but maintained some traditional administrative and other functions

French Enlightenment thinker who believed in the social contract and the concept of the rule of law, which would bring stability to a republic founded on the social contract; influenced the American and French Revolutions

warriors who fought for lords in medieval Europe under the feudal system; were usually rewarded with land and often became lords themselves

Vladimir Lenin

Toussaint L'Ouverture

Berlin Conference

revolutionary Russian socialist; believed in the *dictatorship of the proletariat*, or that socialism required a strong state apparatus; developed Marxism-Leninism; led the Russian Revolution; founder of the Soviet Union

leader of slave rebellion in Haiti, ultimately winning Haitian independence from France in 1791

1884 conference in Berlin where Africa was divided into colonies controlled by European powers as part of the "Scramble for Africa," without regard for Africans

English War

Assyria

Tenochtitlan

1642 conflict between the Royalists, who supported the monarchy, and the Parliamentarians, who wanted a republic

Sumerian-based civilization in the Near East; established military dominance and played an important role in regional trade

capital of the Aztec Empire near modern Mexico City

Charlemagne

humanism

Mali Empire

Frankish (French) leader who united much of Western Europe in the Middle Ages following the chaotic period after the fall of the Roman Empire, leading to more organization and strengthening of the feudal system; crowned emperor in 800 CE

a mode of thought emphasizing human nature, creativity, and an overarching concept of truth; emerged during the European Renaissance

powerful African Islamic empire based at Timbuktu; rich in salt and gold

Nile Valley

Maya

Thirty Years' War

the fertile land on the banks of the Nile River conducive to agriculture and irrigation

dominated the Yucatán Peninsula around 300 CE; had a complex spiritual belief system, detailed calendar, written language, and pyramidal temples; studied astronomy and mathematics

European conflict (1618 – 1648) based on rifts between Protestant and Catholic Christianities and related alliances; outcome reinforced the concept of state sovereignty in Europe

Hundred Years' War

Seven Years' War

Russo-Japanese War

ongoing conflict in Europe during the fourteenth and fifteenth centuries, particularly between England and France; period of political disorganization

first true global conflict (1756 – 1763); conflict among Europeans over control of Habsburg territories; conflict between England and France in North America and Asia for colonial power

1905 defeat of Russia by Japan that cemented Japan's status as an emerging industrial and military world power; signaled decline of imperial Russia

Charles Martel

trench warfare

Hernán Cortés

Frankish (French) leader who stopped Islamic incursions into Europe from Iberia (al Andalus)

bloody, long-term fighting in fortified trenches on the Western Front during World War I

Spanish explorer who captured Aztec ruler Montezuma II and invaded Mexico

English Bill of Rights

Silk Road

Mughal Empire

established constitutional monarchy in England in 1689

term to describe trade routes stretching from Europe to China through Central Asia; spurred global exchange of goods and information

composed of small kingdoms in the Indian subcontinent from the sixteenth century until British rule; influential in Indian Ocean trade routes

Holy Roman Empire

League of Nations

Treaty of Tordesillas

collection of disparate Germanic lands in Central Europe from 962 to 1806

a largely toothless international organization established after WWI and designed to prevent future outbreaks of international war; the basis for the later United Nations

the 1494 treaty that allowed the Portuguese to claim Brazil

concentration camps

Mansa Musa

glasnost

forced labor and death camps where the Nazis imprisoned and killed Jews, Roma and Slavic people, homosexuals, disabled people, people of color, prisoners of war, communists, and others as part of the Holocaust

wealthy and powerful emperor of the Mali Empire; made pilgrimage to Mecca in 1324, showing influence of the empire

Soviet reform meaning "openness"

Middle Ages

printing press

Mecca

time period from the fall of Rome to around the tenth century in Europe

a device that enabled the rapid production and distribution of written manuscripts, thereby spreading information more widely

holy city of Islam; located in the Arabian Peninsula; birthplace of Muhammad

cuneiform

Ninety-Five Theses

Scientific Revolution

a Sumerian development; the earliest-known alphabet

letter of protest written in 1517 to the pope by the monk Martin Luther; expressed dissatisfaction with the state of the Catholic Church; ideas at the heart of the Protestant Reformation

time of scientific exploration and discoveries based in Islamic and ancient Greek and Roman scholarship; threatened the power of the Catholic Church

Julius Caesar

Muhammad

Simón Bolívar

a popular Roman military leader who forced the corrupt Senate to give him control and who began transitioning Rome from a republic to what would become an empire; assassinated in 44 BCE

Arab leader who introduced Islam and led the conquest of the Arabian Peninsula

nineteenth-century revolutionary Latin American leader

First Crusade

ancient Egyptians

Glorious Revolution

invasion of the Holy Land and capture of Jerusalem by European Christians in 1099 in an effort to take the region from Islamic control

emerged as early as 5000 BCE in the Nile Valley; known for their pyramids, art, use of papyrus as paper, and pictorial writing (hieroglyphs); united under one monarch, or pharaoh

the overthrow of Catholic James II by his daughter, Mary II, and her husband, William of Orange; also called the Bloodless Revolution

Mehmed the Conqueror

Voltaire

Church of England

fifteenth-century Ottoman caliph who expanded the empire from Hungary through Mesopotamia

French Enlightenment thinker critical of absolute monarchy, the Catholic Church, and censorship; influenced the French Revolution

Protestant church founded by King Henry VIII; after years of conflict, would become the dominant religion in England

Joan of Arc

euro

Athens

French leader in the 1429 Battle of Orléans; inspired French resistance to English incursions

introduced in 2002, a common currency used in many European countries; globally important

ancient Greek city-state that became a revolutionary democracy controlled by the poor and working classes around 460 BCE; the first known democracy

industrialization

nuclear weapons

"Scramble for Africa"

the process of manufacturing; the process of an economy transforming from dependence on agricultural to industrial production; replacement of hand labor by machines, exponentially increasing production capacities

very powerful weapons that can destroy entire cities; possessed by only a few world powers; first developed by the United States and the Soviet Union

term used to describe rapid nineteenth-century European colonization of Africa; African colonization symbolized power and prestige among European countries

Sumerians

Marie Antoinette

fiefs

ancient Near Eastern people who emerged around 2500 BCE; developed irrigation, agriculture, education, math, astronomy, religion, art, literature, city-states, governance, and administration

unpopular French queen during the French Revolution; symbolic of the nobility's disconnection with and abuse of the people; came under suspicion for her Austrian origins; ultimately arrested and assassinated

territory granted by lords to their vassals in exchange for loyalty under the feudal system

Incas

Moors

Genghis Khan

Andean civilization dominant in western South America before European contact; constructed mountain transportation and agricultural infrastructure

North African Muslims who invaded and settled Iberia (al Andalus)

Mongol leader who led expansion of the Mongol Empire in the twelfth and thirteenth centuries

Mongol Empire

hieroglyphs

Pax Romana

Central Asian empire that dominated most of Eurasia, thanks to the Mongols' equestrian and archery skills and lack of a dominant regional power

ancient Egyptian writing (unlike cuneiform); pictographs, not an alphabet

refers to a period of stability in the Mediterranean region under the Roman Empire

Babylonia

Montesquieu

"White Man's Burden"

Sumerian-based civilization in Mesopotamia; developed courts and an early codified rule of law—the Code of Hammurabi

French Enlightenment thinker who introduced the idea of the separation of powers, an important element of American democracy

an 1899 poem written by British novelist Rudyard Kipling to encourage the United States to engage in a war with the Philippines, joining the nations of Western Europe in fulfilling (in their minds) their "burden" to "civilize" nonwhites around the world; term generally refers to the racist idea that Western whites are "superior" to the rest of the world and must control it for the good of all, which informed imperialism

League of Nations

Martin Luther

Reformation

an international organization founded after World War I dedicated to the preservation of peace in the world based on Woodrow Wilson's Fourteen Points

Catholic monk who wrote a letter of protest to the pope in 1517 known as the Ninety-Five Theses

movement for reform of the Catholic Church; resulted in new factions of Christianity in Europe

John Locke

apartheid

Enlightenment

Enlightenment thinker who believed in the social contract: in exchange for protection and to enjoy social benefits, people relinquish some sovereignty to a republican government; influenced the American Revolution

oppressive social system in South Africa that separated people by race in public places; led to structural inequalities and lowered standard of living for people of color; lasted for most of the twentieth century

the basis for reinvigorated European culture and political thought beginning around the eighteenth century that would drive European development and influence in later countries like the United States

Ottoman Empire

Meiji Restoration

European Union

Turkic empire that controlled Anatolia, the Balkans, and eventually the Middle East and much of the Mediterranean world; Ottomans captured Istanbul, capital of the Ottoman Empire, in 1453

period of technological and military modernization in Japan beginning in 1868; helped Japan become an important military power

a forum for European countries to organize and cooperate politically, militarily, and economically; formed after the Cold War to promote European unity

OPEC

Augustus Caesar

perestroika

an intergovernmental organization founded in 1960 composed of the thirteen (originally five) largest petroleum-exporting countries; an important influence on the global economy

Julius Caesar's nephew Octavian, who gained control of Rome in 27 BCE and became the first Roman emperor; associated with a time of expansion and stability

literally meaning "restructuring," the movement led by Mikhail Gorbachev to liberalize the Soviet Union's command economy

Suleiman the Magnificent

Forbidden City

pharaoh

sixteenth-century Ottoman caliph who consolidated Ottoman rule throughout the Mediterranean world

imposing home of the Chinese emperor in Beijing; constructed under the Ming dynasty

ancient Egyptian monarch

Estates-General

Franco-Prussian War

Reconquista

the weak representative governing assembly under the French king; included the clergy, the nobility, and the Third Estate (the middle class and the poor peasants); convened in an unsuccessful effort to resolve fiscal crisis prior to the outbreak of the French Revolution

1870 conflict in which Prussia began to assert its military power and took control of mineral-rich Alsace-Lorraine from France; outcome helped fuel Prussian industrial development

Christian raids of Islamic Spain (al-Andalus); expulsion of Islamic powers from Iberia; and unification of Christian kingdoms in Spain into one Christian kingdom

Bastille

Otto von Bismarck

Montezuma II

a Paris prison that represented tyranny before the French Revolution; stormed in a revolutionary act on July 14, 1789, when the king sent troops to Paris

Prussian leader who consolidated the linguistically and culturally Germanic Central European states of Prussia into the German Empire in 1871

Aztec leader when Europeans arrived in Mesoamerica; captured by Spanish explorer Hernán Cortés

Second Industrial Revolution

Great Leap Forward

Atahualpa

occurred in the late nineteenth and early twentieth centuries; based on heavy industry, railroads, and weapons

Mao Zedong's plan to modernize the Chinese economy, which was scheduled to last from 1958 – 1963 but ended with Mao's resignation in 1960

the last independent Inca emperor, defeated by Francisco Pizarro in 1533

Iranian Revolution

Non-Aligned Movement

decolonization

1979 overthrow of the shah, resulting in the establishment of a theocracy in Iran hostile to US interests

organized coalition of countries unaligned with the US or the USSR; also called the Third World; many countries were formerly European colonies

Decolonization was the twentieth-century process by which European colonial hegemony was ended in African, Asian, and Middle Eastern territories, and those areas became independent countries. Despite UN leadership and efforts, at times the process became violent.

pan-Arabism

Arab nationalist movement throughout the ethnic Arab and Arabic-speaking world; one driving force of the Arab-Israeli conflict

Government

sovereignty

rule of law

the right of a group to be free of outside interference

laws that would apply to all equally and would equally benefit all

social contract

popular sovereignty

John Locke

Individuals turn over certain individual sovereignty to a neutral party (a government), which holds the responsibility to maximize the individual enjoyment of rights as well as the public good.

Government obtains legitimacy only with the consent of the people.

an influential Enlightenment thinker best known for his concept of natural rights and his writings on the social contract

legitimacy

demokratia

liberals

recognition of a government's authority

ancient Greek word meaning "people power"; root of the English word *democracy*

In the United States, liberals tend to believe in the power and responsibility of government to effect positive change.

conservatives

libertarianism

Articles of Confederation

In the United States, conservatives tend to believe in the individual's (and private sector's) power and responsibility to effect positive change.

a political ideology on the far right of the political spectrum that supports an extremely limited government, rejecting any kind of government social programs and any government intervention in the market

the first governing document drawn up by the Second Continental Congress for the new nation in 1781

Constitution

Declaration of the Rights of Man and the Citizen

expressed powers or enumerated powers

the document that provides the framework for the US government

precursor to the revolutionary French constitution ensuring liberty and equality; written in the model of Enlightenment thought

powers that are specifically granted to the federal government only

reserved powers

implied powers

inherent powers

powers that are held by the states through the Tenth Amendment, which states that all powers not expressly given to the federal government belong to the states

powers held by the federal government that are not in the Constitution; derive from the Elastic Clause of the Constitution

powers that derive specifically from US sovereignty and are inherent to its existence as a nation, like making treaties or waging war

concurrent powers

prohibited powers

Congress

powers that are shared equally by both the national and state governments, such as levying taxes or establishing courts

powers that are denied to both the national government and the state governments

the branch of the federal government that makes laws (the legislative branch); technically, it has the most power in government; composed of the House of Representatives and the Senate

House of Representatives

proportional representation

Speaker of the House

the body of lawmakers in Congress with proportional representation reflecting the population of each state

The number of representatives from each state is based on the state's population (as in the House of Representatives).

the leader of the House of Representatives; also the leader of the majority party in the House

Senate

president

vice president

the upper house of Congress; the body of lawmakers in Congress with equal representation—two senators are elected to represent each state; also refers to the governing body of republican ancient Rome upon which the US body was modeled

the head of state and head of the executive branch; has the power to appoint federal officials and judges, to sign or veto laws (approve or deny them), and to make foreign policy; he or she is also the commander-in-chief of the US armed forces

fulfills the duties of the president when he or she is unable; becomes president in the event of the president's death; also serves as president of the Senate

separation of powers

Supremacy Clause

Equal Protection Clause

the foundational philosophy of the structure of the American government that requires the division of government powers among multiple branches (specifically three), with each branch having the power to check the other branches

Article VI, Clause 2 of the Constitution, which states that the Constitution is the "supreme law of the land"

in Section 1 of the Fourteenth Amendment to the Constitution, originally created to ensure the equal treatment of blacks under the law

Establishment Clause

Free Exercise Clause

Elastic Clause

in the First Amendment, prohibits the government from establishing a state religion or favoring one religion over another

in the First Amendment, prohibits the government from restricting religious belief

Article I, Section 8 of the Constitution; gives Congress the right to make all laws "necessary and proper" for carrying out other powers (granting implied powers)

impeachment

veto

pocket veto

formally accusing an official of wrongdoing

when the president prevents a bill from becoming law after it has passed through both houses of Congress

occurs when there are less than ten days in a congressional session and the president does not sign a bill, causing it to die

judicial review

taxes

political action committee

the power held by the Supreme Court to determine the constitutionality of laws

money paid by the people, organizations, and companies to the government

committees formed by interest groups with the express purpose of raising money in support of specific candidates running for public office

gerrymandering

direct primary

unitary government

when political parties attempt to create congressional districts to ensure the maximum number of seats for their party, maximizing power

a method of selecting candidates for each party in which voters (who are not necessarily registered members of the party, depending on the state) vote for their preferred candidate, sometimes choosing from a group of several running for office

a government in which all power is vested in the central governments, rather than being distributed among or shared with regional governments

multiparty system

realism

Fourth Amendment

a political system in which there are several different political parties vying for, and ultimately sharing, power

a theory of international relations articulated by Hans J. Morgenthau, which posits that a state's primary interest is self-preservation, and this can be achieved only by maximizing power

restricts unlawful searches and seizures

Fifth Amendment

Miranda rights

Sixth Amendment

protects the accused from self-incrimination

the due process rights required to be made known to those arrested before interrogation

guarantees the accused the right to a fair, speedy, and public trial, as well as the right to counsel in criminal cases (which can be provided by the government)

Thirteenth Amendment

Fourteenth Amendment

civil rights

prohibited slavery in the United States; ratification was required for reentry into the Union after the Civil War

ratified in 1868; original purpose was to ensure the equal treatment of African Americans under the law after the abolition of slavery; since then, the Equal Protection Clause has been used to protect civil rights

protections against discriminatory treatment by the government of individuals of a variety of groups

Geography

physical geography

absolute location

the study of the natural processes of the earth

a location that is described by its position on Earth without referencing landmarks

relative location

spatial relationships

cardinal directions

where a place is situated in relation to another place or places

how one place is located in relation to another place

north, south, east, and west

intermediate directions

regions

natural resources

the directions between the cardinal directions

parts of the world with definable and identifiable characteristics

fresh water, arable land, fuel, livestock, and game

conformal map

high latitudes

middle latitudes

a map that maintains the accuracy of the shape of areas on the earth while distorting size

latitudes from 66.5° north and south to the poles

the region located from latitudes 23.5° to 66.5° north and south

low latitudes

climate

humid continental climate

the region located from the equator to latitudes 23.5° north and south

the average weather for a location or region

located in the middle latitudes, the agriculturally productive, true four-season climate

Mediterranean climate

marine climate

desert

a climate located in the middle latitudes between latitudes 30° and 40° north and south characterized by wet, mild winters and dry, warm summers

the warm and rainy climate located in the middle latitudes in areas that are near or surrounded by water

a climate located in the low latitudes north and south of the savannah; receives less than 10 inches of rainfall a year; the hottest and driest parts of the earth

humid subtropical climate

savannah

steppes or prairie

located in the middle latitudes, a warm and moist climate on coastal areas north and south of the tropics that receive warm ocean currents and warm winds year round

a climate located in the low latitudes north and south of the rainforest; dry in the winter and wet in the summer, experiencing an average of 10 to 30 inches of rain

a climate located in the middle latitudes far from the ocean, characterized by flatlands and minimal rainfall

tropical rainforests

tundra

taiga

moist forests exhibiting high biodiversity, located mainly in the equatorial lowlands in Central Africa, Southeast Asia, and the Amazon basin

a cold climate located in the high latitudes north of the taiga; with extremely cold and long winters, the ground is frozen for most of the year and becomes mushy during the short summer

a cold climate located in the high latitudes south of the tundra; contains the world's largest forestlands, extreme mineral wealth, and many swamps and marshes

human geography

social structures

culture complex

the study of the impact of people on the physical world

the organization of a society and how social events relate to and affect places

the sum of a place's or region's cultural traits (the various single aspects of its culture)

carrying capacity

geographic features

migration

the number of people a place or a region can support

physical features of a place like continents, bodies of water, plains, plateaus, mountains, and valleys

patterns of movement from one place to another with the intention of settling permanently at the new location

urban planning

purchasing power parity

primate city

managing the development and use of cities

an exchange rate that determines equivalence between the spending powers of currency in different countries

a city that has a disproportionate concentration of a state's resources

contagious diffusion

migration stream

possibilism

a pattern of the spread of culture in which the hearth, or the original location of the phenomenon, is surrounded by multiple places that adopt the phenomenon at the same time

the spatial movement of a migration from its place of origin to the location of its destination

a theory of human-environment interaction that states that humans have a greater role in shaping the structure and nature of their culture than environment does

political features

shifting cultivation

agricultural location theory

towns and cities; county, state, or national borders

a practice of subsistence farming in which farmers rotate the types of crops grown in each field in order to preserve the health of the soil

examines how distance impacts location decisions in agriculture; developed by Johann Heinrich von Thünen

globalization

urbanization

suburbanization

the process of businesses, technologies, and belief systems spreading across the globe

the movement of people from rural areas to urban settings to live and work; began during the Industrial Revolution when unskilled jobs in factories attracted rural workers, who could make higher wages

the movement of urban dwellers from cities to live in growing suburbs: semirural areas at the outskirts of cities

human capital

technology

interdependence

the knowledge and skills of the labor force

a nation's knowledge and ability to efficiently produce goods

being part of a larger global or regional economy

multinational corporations (MNCs)

demography

birth rate or crude birth rate (CBR)

companies based in one country with operations in one or more other countries; major driving forces of globalization

the quantitative study of social change, involving statistical review

a demographic determinant that measures the number of births per thousand in the population per year

death rate or crude death rate (CDR)

Demographic Transition Model

rate of natural increase (RNI)

a demographic determinant that concerns the number of deaths per thousand in a given population per year

a geographic tool that predicts changes in population using the crude birth rate (CBR), crude death rate (CDR), and the rate of natural increase (RNI)

how much the population is increasing based on the crude birth rate (CBR) and crude death rate (CDR)

Economics

supply

demand

how much of a product or service the market can offer

how much desire there is for a product or service

scarcity

choice

utility

the limited amount of available resources

selecting one want over another

the point of greatest economic happiness or satisfaction

elasticity

opportunity cost

marginal benefit

the measure of sensitivity to change; economists use price elasticity of demand and price elasticity of supply to measure economic change

the value (cost) of the opportunity lost by choosing another opportunity in its place

the additional benefit

marginal cost

economic growth

absolute advantage

the additional cost

increase in production of goods and services over time; the expansion of a production possibilities curve, or frontier, over time

when an individual, company, or country can produce a good or service more efficiently than all competitors in that market

comparative advantage

specialization

price

when an individual, company, or country can produce one good or service more efficiently than it can produce another good or service; the comparison of the opportunity costs of production for two different producers

when an individual, company, or country focuses on producing one product or service, typically because it has a comparative advantage

the primary communication tool of the market; indicates the relative value of products

law of demand

law of supply

equilibrium

As the price for a good or service increases, the demand for it will decrease, if all other factors remain constant.

As the price of a good increases, suppliers will increase the quantity of the good they supply, if all other factors remain constant.

state of the market when the quantity demanded equals the quantity supplied at a given price; both suppliers and buyers are satisfied with the price; represented on a graph at the point where the supply and demand curves intersect

shortage or excess demand

surplus or excess supply

public goods

when the quantity demanded of a good or service exceeds the quantity supplied

when the quantity supplied exceeds the quantity demanded

products that can be consumed without reducing their availability to other consumers and that are equally available to all; examples include sewage infrastructure and basic television

firm

short term

long term

any organization that uses factors of production to produce a good or service that it intends to sell for profit

in economics, a period of time in which at least one production input is fixed and cannot be changed

in economics, a period of time in which all production inputs are changeable

law of diminishing returns

gross domestic product (GDP)

Consumer Price Index (CPI)

when the value of benefits or profit is less than the amount of energy or investment required to attain them

the total value of all the final goods and services produced within a nation in one year

measures prices of goods and services as they change over time

inflation

traditional economy

pure command economy

the percent increase in the Consumer Price Index from year to year

a pre-industrialized economy, guided by tradition, often using bartering rather than currency

usually found in communist societies; the government, rather than the market, determines all aspects of production; rarely found today (one example is North Korea)

pure market economy

mixed economy

economic regulation

also known as capitalism; governed by the laws of supply and demand; no outside (government) interference

controlled by both the market and the government; defines most modern economies

indirect or direct price control by the government

relative price of a good

increasing marginal costs

What is price elasticity of demand?

the value of the good in relation to other items of similar value

the rise of the marginal costs of production as suppliers increase the amount they are supplying

the measurement of the extent to which changes in price alter demand; represented by the following equation:

E_d = % of change in quantity demanded/% of change in price

demand curve

supply curve

allocation of resources

a graphic economic model that shows how demand changes as prices increase; measures quantity demanded in relation to price

a graphic economic model that shows the relationship between what a product or service costs and how much a business is willing to supply for sale (price and quantity)

how resources are distributed across an economy

fiscal policy

monetary stabilization

expansionary fiscal policy

refers to the means by which a government manages the economy

efforts to keep fiscal indicators like prices, unemployment, and the money supply relatively stable

government action to expand the amount of money in the economy

maximizing utility

substitution effect

sole proprietorship

achieving the point of greatest happiness or satisfaction (in making economic choices)

the choice by consumers to purchase cheaper products when prices rise

a business belonging to a single individual

partnership

corporation

economies of scale

a joint venture between two individuals or two business entities

a group of individuals or businesses working together to share business risk and profit

the reduction in costs resulting from increasing production of a product, allowing the per unit cost to be spread out over an increasing number of units

diseconomies of scale

perfect or pure competition

monopoly

when a firm's expansion hurts profit

when no one business controls the entire marketplace

the control of a market for a good or service by one company or group

Sociology

functionalism

ethnocentrism

the category of social perspective based on the interconnectedness of modern society

the belief that one's culture and ethnicity is superior to all others

looking-glass self

secondary socialization

conflict

the theory of socialization that states that people build their own self-images through the ways in which others perceive them; posited by C.H. Cooley

the process of learning the appropriate behaviors, attitudes, and values to have as a member of a subgroup within the larger society

the process of disagreement, usually resolved when one of the parties receives either the entirety or a satisfactory amount of the desired goal

cooperation

exchange

network

the process of working together to achieve similar goals; often leads to positive outcomes

the process of social interaction in which one individual or group gives something to another group or individual, who then gives something else in return

a relationship, based on shared interest or purpose, that grows among individuals or organizations

institutions

primary socialization

social class

extensions of core social values created in response to varying individual and group needs; includes government, private enterprise, religious and academic institutions, local communities, and the family unit

when a child learns the values, actions, and attitudes that are appropriate for his or her culture

refers to the arrangement of relative positions in society

power

prestige

status

the capacity to exert influence over others; in sociology, often relates to relationships among and within social classes

the general admiration of a person or a group of people based on the appearance of success or achievement

how individuals are viewed in the world

nationalism

vertical mobility

prejudice

sentiment of loyalty to one's own cultural or ethnic group above others

a type of social mobility in which an individual moves from one social level to another

pre-judgments of an individual or group based off of stereotypes

discrimination

inequality

positive deviance

action taken based on prejudices

the result of discrimination

an approach to the study of behavioral difference that examines the impact of uncommon but successful behaviors of individuals or small subgroups of the larger society

organic solidarity

ethnomethodology

socialization

a form of social cohesion that occurs in societies where individuals are interconnected on a broad level but are more specifically motivated by individual interests

a theoretical perspective developed by Harold Garfinkel that attempts to explain how people interpret their own actions in the world

a process whereby individuals learn skills, beliefs, values, and behavior patterns of society and how these can influence their own norms and customs

social stigma

What are the main factors of social change?

an attribute of behavior or reputation used to socially discredit a group or beliefs

Social change is based on external causes, internal causes, technological advancements, and social movements.

Psychology

critical period

accommodation

a period of development in which certain skills are acquired

the process of adjusting schemata to incorporate new, contradictory information

scaffold

operant conditioning

classical conditioning

a process used to help children acquire new skills by providing assistance or guided steps

a process of learning in which consequences are associated with behaviors; B. F. Skinner coined the term

when a subject learns to respond to a neutral stimulus in the same way it responds to a reflexive stimulus by associating the two

reinforcement

punishment

semantic network

a consequence that makes a behavior more likely

the opposite of reinforcement; it decreases the likelihood of a behavior by providing unpleasant consequences for a response

a web of interconnected memories in the brain that assists in information retrieval

memory consolidation

superego

determinism

the process by which neurons create connections across the brain to allow for more efficient access to memories

according to Sigmund Freud's psychoanalytic approach to personality theory, the part of the self that helps a person determine right from wrong

the idea that personality is determined by past events

nomothetic theory

perceived control

attitude

a category of personality theory; argues that a set number of traits can be used to describe all personalities

an individual's feeling of control over a stressor in his or her life

an evaluative set of beliefs and feelings shaped by perceptions of and interaction with people, places, and things

fundamental attribution error

bystander effect

extrinsic motivator

when people give undue credit to a person rather than to a situation for a person's action or behavior

the tendency of people to allow wrongdoing when they are part of a crowd of witnesses

a motivator for behavior that comes from outside the self

intrinsic motivator

perceive

maturation

a motivator for behavior that comes from within the self

to interpret sensory information

the biological process of aging

the Moro reflex

the Babinski reflex

social psychology

a startle reflex in which a baby throws its arms out and pulls them back

a reflex in infants; a baby extends its big toe when the bottom of the foot is touched

the study of how people relate to each other

social cognition

exposure effect

the application of cognition concepts to individuals' conceptions of themselves and others

the idea that the more someone is exposed to something, the more he or she will like it

Made in the USA
Middletown, DE
16 November 2017